Borrowed
Andrea Holland

Smith/Doorstop Books

Published 2007 by
Smith/Doorstop Books
The Poetry Business
The Studio
Byram Arcade
Westgate
Huddersfield HD1 1ND

Copyright © Andrea Holland 2007
All Rights Reserved

ISBN 978-1-902382-91-3
Typeset at The Poetry Business
Printed by Swiftprint, Huddersfield

The Poetry Business gratefully acknowledges the help of Arts Council England and Kirklees Metropolitan Council.

Acknowledgements
Many thanks to the editors of the following, in which some of these poems first appeared: *The North, Reactions, Reactions 2, Reactions 4, The Rialto, roger (USA), Smith's Knoll*

This collection was a winner in The Poetry Business
Book & Pamphlet Competition 2006

CONTENTS

5	On Not Writing a Villanelle
6	Borrowed
8	New Year's Eve
9	Return Home by Weeping-Cross
10	Calefaction
11	Solitude (the Library Book)
17	Four Miniatures by John Smart (1741-1811)
18	On Hearing a Jazz Trio play *Smells like Teen Spirit* by Nirvana
19	Self Burial, 1969
20	Rockpool
21	Delivery
22	On Diane Arbus and her *Albino Sword Swallower at a Carnival*
23	Rochester's Suitcase
24	Turn
25	Darling, Meet me in Language
26	I'm looking at a Sunflower, lopsided

*for Austin and Caleb:
kings of east anglia*

ON NOT WRITING A VILLANELLE

*I do not want to make a stone horse
that is trying to and cannot smell the air,*
said Barbara Hepworth, the woman who disappears in fire.

There is a woman who disappears in fire
every time the sun drops over the stairs
of her studio, as she makes a stone horse

which does not look like a stone horse:
she's all for abstraction, the sculpted mare
will look like solid wood as it disappears in fire.

In the Cornish garden, bronze sculptures disappear in fire
as the sun burns through the greenhouse, on the Maidenhair
fern and Bougainvillea beneath the glass. A stone horse

among the flowers, she gets it right, a stone horse
which breathes among flowers, in a lair
of Angel's trumpets. The pollen disappears in fire

as a fat bee glows like a coal disappearing into fire.
It spreads the pollen and goes home, where
something happens and honey is made; as a stone horse

is sculpted, something happens. The woman, a stone horse,
the studio all burn up, there's no air
left to breathe: eyes, nostrils, hair – it all disappears in fire.

BORROWED

Pigeons, the colour of London, stuttering down
to the parked car, a white Hillman. A Tippex white (or has
that not been invented?) car, and city pigeons. I should mention

> Victoria Station but that is less clear than the woman
> with fists, white hands beating on the window
> of the little Hillman, with shouts like *give her to me, get her out*

right now. From inside it is like talking under water. The white rage
of the woman thumping the glass like a manoeuvre
for resuscitation – the whites of her eyes through the, white

> sun light, window. A pigeon distracts me when it swerves
> by the woman who is shouting at the man inside. He holds my hand
> and grips the gear shift with the other hand. To the woman

outside the window in a white blouse, one collarbone visible,
the man at the wheel is wicked for keeping me inside when,
clearly, I am hers. I keep seeing this one pigeon with a piece of white

> bread in its broken claw. It's half hopping and pecking and
> I can't meet its eye. People pass the woman and the white
> car and pretend they don't see what's happening. Now

she is cooling down – no more crackling like a white sheet
on the washing line. I hear the word *please* and my father,
it is my father, takes his eyes off the white dial on the dash-

> board and a hand moves from the gear stick to the little knob
> by the window which keeps my mother out and me with
> him. An announcement for a train, a voice I think I recognise,

like our neighbours in the painted white house, a departing train.
My mother reaches in and I see the white pearl of her earring
like an eye as she lifts me up towards the white sun of her blouse.

    The pigeons billow out and up in a grey wave in the wake of the white car. The man who looks like a ghost at the wheel, takes a white handkerchief from his top pocket and wipes at the window until we are gone.

NEW YEAR'S EVE

It's no small thing
to negate the stars, the very stars
which guide us. Where you are you forget
to breathe now and then. Look up.
Some reckless constellation is still holding on,
I've got you.

There's a place where conversations go
when we are sleeping. Come back
from your head to me. Up ahead
a child is dreaming of balloons
blue as a robin's egg. He was a tiny star
in your blackness, now he is a robin's egg.
Don't let go,
Don't ever let go.

The moon is the same moon.
This tide is the same tide.
This is why we continue, why we believe.
The baby on your lap is sleeping, little bird,
eyes black as stars, all yours. Here we are
then, where we talk and the lick of moon
rises.

RETURN HOME BY WEEPING-CROSS

> *'To return home by weeping-cross': to repent sorrowfully having taken a certain course –*
> Dictionary of the English Language, 1897

Summer stacked in raw fields – that is straw.
It is blond, dry, animal food.
Straw towers wrapped in black plastic,
like a roof, for protection.
And yet look how hay houses are rained into ruin.

So then you build with sticks, which are not worth much
more than straw. What good but in the burning?
And, here, I burnt other things besides – spindly kindling
the least best thing. I burnt my mouth.
You, by degrees.

And so to bricks. Red bricks as bold as love.
Who needs timber, with all its hesitation
and rot? Bricks, mortar – of these a home
is made. We go inside to be warm. We go
out and forget the key. But that is not
where I went wrong: I blew down every house
you built. I return home, lupine, each night
by weeping cross.

CALEFACTION

I kissed the plumber today, a smackaroo –
I suppose it won't do, what with the kids
in the next room listening to the radio,
Radio 2. You'll say something about my age,
the scene; like a Carry-On flick, a window
cleaner's saucy dream…
But I know I'm the Queen of Romance:
his tongue in my mouth still warm
from the coffee I just served, milky
and sweet. He drank it fast, in the kitchen,
watching me cook tea; his filthy hands
wrapped tight as insulation around
the cracked mug, his thumb across Lady
Di's lips, her eyeliner black as smut, not yet
smudged by tears.

SOLITUDE (THE LIBRARY BOOK)

*From March 1974 to May 1999, thirteen stamps of issue
in a library copy of* Walden

> *'I never found the companion that was so companionable
> as solitude'* – Henry D Thoreau

29 March 1974
Spring snow unfurled and quilting the field; a solitary
dog sniffs out a stick to chew. It is a word picked
from a white page.(Iced snow clots
the rim of his brown paws.) The stick, wet
and split, in his black jaw: the memory of bone.

10 June
and tadpoles are growing legs. The pond water begins
to move with Waterboatmen. Ants orienteer the crease
of an open book. Say, *Leaves of Grass*: *mind how
once we lay such a transparent summer morning.*
But witness a self as a self only and not part of another, no illusion
of other, no Narcissus. The comfort of pages, the company of bugs.
Somewhere else, a dog shakes water out of himself
in a shudder like sex. Remember the shaking, the letting go.

This morning a mist of heat lifted from the water
like a veil and the show began. A one-man show.

28 April 1975
The curiosity of a stray dog is like quicksand: don't stand still
for too long, take a good look around. Eyes button black,
black as two ellipses, something left out of the line on a page.

Eyes fix on a rabbit. Rabbits ring the field like flotsam.
A dog can't help but pursue. No one to call him back, no one
to say his name, to command or plead *Come here, Come back*.
Punishment is not the same as not getting the rabbit. It's only April.

5 August
There is a part of the woods that leads to the Rappahanock river
in Stafford County, Virginia, called PhoneBook. This is the name
two boys gave the place one morning in August 1975. Their Dad
parked the truck facing the water, but in a river of yellow pages
ripped from a directory. Black and yellow plague of paper poised
at the water's edge, like a thirsty dog, some others blowing
in the little available air, small ghosts of information (The Mane Frame
beauty salon, tool hire, funeral directors, all scrambled and more limp
by the minute.) Someone has ripped apart a phone book in these
woods. How strong do you have to be to tear apart
a phone book? Imagine Thoreau walking in Walden, amongst
these pages. Imagine tearing apart a directory like rending
garments in grief. Boys swim in the river, which moves with
dragonflies and paper. A man at the shore sits and writes
something down on a blank white square of his notebook.
One thing to notice is how the pages of the phone book
look like fallen leaves. The tree is a telegraph pole. The river
in August is the one place to go to cool off, to let off steam.

16 October 1976
Fall, and you read about safety pins
through the ears of kids in England.
It is the American bicentennial and nothing
could be further from the filth
and fury of the Thames. Here is a big plain
of red and white and blue. Celebrate leaving
the motherland and WonderWoman's

bikini. Angels are not in their heaven, some
are cocaine, some on television, or in the memory
of a glade of bluebells in Sussex. And in the white
spaces between the dark lines of Thoreau's
book of notes. Notes like pinned insects
in the wood, lines on a tree, small black strands
of graffiti on a torched car: it is written, *no future*.

19 May 1978
Sparrows raindance along the shorn hedge
of a field. Thoreau considers them purfling,
thinks of them as decorating the border
of this field like muddy lace. The earth has been
ploughed into itself like a frozen wave. Stopped
dead in its tracks. A rabbit bloodied by a fox
has oiled the upturned soil with its blood.
This is Thoreau's purlieu, the edges of the world,
one man's May Day.

5 November 1979
My father ran the firework display
and for months before we turned our thoughts
to pennies for the Guy, the fiery devices
lived in a trunk inside our house. At night
I heard arguments, bargaining, and concessions:
I trusted you. Children in purdah listening
to the humming of radiators, pipes flaring up,
the boiler sparking to life. The room spun
like a Catherine Wheel and the volume
was too high. In the morning we stormed
the school field looking for left over fireworks,
for the paper parachutes which brought some

back to earth. The paper too scorched
and thin to hold anything. I always think,
if I ever meet someone who has leapt
from a plane, I would ask them what they thought:
Is it a question of, will this thing hold me up,
or is it knowing when to jump?

22 July 1982
Alone, lonely, lonesome, solitary. These adjectives
are compared as they describe lack of companionship.
Alone emphasizes being apart from others but does not
necessarily imply unhappiness. Thoreau's dictionary
says so. Out of the damp window of his cabin, Thoreau
spots magpies in the field, *Pica pica*, black bird with tin
foil in its beak. Shiny gobstopper for the nest; to show
off with. One for sorrow, two for joy, three for a girl,
four for a boy. Thoreau claps his hands and the bird
rises up in a bright but noiseless arc. A brown dog
barks at the closed door and it opens. He is welcome,
he is company, he is alone.

11 December 1985
Looking over the shoulder of the year: birds don't dare
stop for too long. Birds on the telegraph wire like musical
notes. Take the phone off the hook and walk past
the mistletoe of Christmas. Walk into the fresh snow of New Year
with a book like a flask against your breast, to look forward to.
To stop and take a little something from.

26 January 1987
A dog is shot dead in the woods. A brindle greyhound

mistaken for a deer. A pack of hunters gather at the body
and laugh awkwardly at the mistake like a surprise party.
A solitary man carries the dog to the nearest house, strong
as Hansel at the witch's door. By the time he returns
to the merry men they are baiting a small fire. The corkscrew hazel
hangs like hundreds of tiny nooses above their heads.
The corkscrew hazel drops like question marks along the words
tracked over a white page. Muddy footprints in the snow.

18 April 1990
means dogwood and lilacs. Thoreau fills his round hat
with glossy blooms and whistles like a Jay, to no-one
in particular. Perhaps a note in the notebook after lunch.

16 October 1993
Trees reinvent themselves as sticks praising
an empty sky. Leaves let go, settling into damp
and mud around the water like easy conversation.
Imagine Walden here in Virginia. Imagine
the rhododendrons blooming livid pink above
the dead pup you buried in a box, in the mud.
The small bones and wet fur clamber through
the layers of cardboard, leaves, silt, sludge
and water. Everything goes ground ward,
everything's ground down to its barest, briefest
essential.

8 May 1999
You've got to write what you remember: Dvorak
in Spillville, writing notes on the starched cuffs
of his white shirts while Native Americans danced

their dance to the earth. Write a letter: *Dear Mister
Thoreau, I am alone in these woods, what shall I do?
Yours most sincerely.* If he wrote back he might tell
you something of himself, something about the green
of lichen, moss, fern leaf and musty pages in a book
long forgotten in a library. A book not much of any use,
not worth stopping for. You stopped and found it;
the words in need of conversation.
Some pages are dog-eared and you save
them for last, for the last light before the journey home.
No doubt you'll return, like a library book lent
for the duration, like a dog who knows he belongs.

FOUR MINIATURES BY JOHN SMART (1741-1811)

1. *Mr Ridley*
    Eyes like chestnuts. Avuncular.
    Wears less powder in his hair than his mother
    thinks he ought. Never beats his dog or kills foxes.
    Admits to himself the tender melancholy of the body
    when alone, undressed for a bath.

2. *Mr Harris*
    His dimpled stubby chin reveals a man not much
    taken with morning or its petty ablutions. Reads
    the Bible to his children with a scowl; faith stronger
    than paternity.

3. *Mr Gemmell*
    Like a ghost, transparent and oblique.
    Friends speak well of him but know not much
    beyond the obvious surface gestures. A gentleman,
    to be sure, but the creases around his eyes are not from
    smiling.

4. *Unknown*
    A man unfinished. Lips like halves of a plum, but never
    seen kissed. He takes the hands of ladies at dances
    but will not marry. Eyes warm, applegreen.
    At the glance of a valet or stable hand he smiles.

ON HEARING A JAZZ TRIO PLAY *SMELLS LIKE TEEN SPIRIT* BY NIRVANA

I just turned on the radio, I'm washing up.
Make that, doing the dishes. This band comes on
and I don't know who it is but I start to recognise
the tune, only they've looped it out, slung it like a lasso

round the saddle of the song. I'm starting
to like how the bass bends the bit where
Kurt Cobain sings *here we are now,
entertain us*. The drums too, are doing something

weird, something almost out of sync. Suddenly
it all sounds rather Swedish. The melody's been pushed
around, an amiable steering as if, left as it was,
it might come to harm, something might go

terribly wrong. It's so quiet in here after the piano
sings *hello, hello, hello, hello.*

SELF BURIAL, 1969

From a photograph by Keith Arnatt

I was led here, it's true. But I am willing.
Each day I am muddled into the earth,
disappearing like a bombed-out city,
like Dresden. It's important you see me
go like this: I've come here to let go
of gravity – my feet are tired like donkeys
at the beach; always the endless back
and forth. The weight of the body.

In winter, in places too cold to stand,
wild horses lie deep in the snow:
they go down into the drifts, become
invisible and stay warm. I look also
to moles, earthworms, the hare
and the fox. I see rabbits go down
into the good earth. I don't eat. I want
for nothing.

I am leaving behind a scar on the land,
a scratch of soil, but you'll find no
reminder. This is not semaphore,
nor loss. There's nothing left to say.
You have to let me go.

ROCKPOOL

Erosion brought us here, to this minute world;
microcosm of the sea, contained by land.
>   There are limpets on limpets and mussels like wings
>   as if the rock which has fallen from the cliff
>   might be lifted back.
Tiny creatures burrow down in the pool's shadows,
leaving sandy trails like comets in the dark corners
>   of this cosmos – they have purpose, direction.
>   This is home. We are fishing around with small green
>   nets, breaking things, changing the set.
The blue mussels close as we touch them, each sea anemone
we graze retracts as if sore. Our playground, this.
>   But the waves' applause grows louder and everything
>   must go. The tide will take us all away on waves
>   rising like dark wings; they close over this little world.
Except for the rocks, faithless and stock-still, we are all
pulled back by the moon.

DELIVERY

The midwife is on her throne.
The word comes from the German,
with wife. But she will not get down,
a regular Marie Antoinette. And who
will feed the chickens? Put my gas mask
on? All that is left is stale bread while
the roof collapses. Everyone says *breathe*
and everyone is wrong. I hold my breath
and see all the stars from this broken
and half empty house.

ON DIANE ARBUS AND HER *ALBINO SWORD SWALLOWER AT A CARNIVAL*

Born under a surgical lamp like a spotlight:
translucent skin, her eyes pale
and fluttering like sick birds. At school

this one stood in the shade of a sycamore tree
and blinked like an owl. Her classmates whispered
and jostled together, played *Red Light Green Light*,

afraid to touch her: a sugar mouse, a doll in thin
clothes, fading. But in her room at home she read
books about Princess Bea and her magical powers,

Princess Bea and her long sunlight hair. She practised
in the yard and insects curled as they flew by, stunned
by the heat in her. This girl bought a trick sword

to swallow; this girl bought a trick sword and swallowed;
this girl swallowed her sword and its shadow
passed down her beautiful clear throat

like a sentence – a language of clarity
lost in the dark world outside.

ROCHESTER'S SUITCASE

is tawny leather, scratched. Unlocked but strapped
down with a belt. Opened like an avocado,
striped silk lines the skin like wallpaper. Wrapped
inside are letters, tied up, and books no
one recalls holding. The bundled letters
are mostly airmail, blue and light as skin.
In opening this case you begin a better
way of looking at the past – you see in,
through the mouth of it. One envelope falls
from the pile, like a playing card, a trick
of the light. The words spell danger, call
out *stop* if you don't want to know the sick
part of your history: a little sin, a life
wrecked, ink wedded to the paper; a prior wife.

TURN

Listen up. Your face is becoming
my face, is relaxing into itself. I think
you want to kiss me. Someone
is hammering at the side, no, the front
of the house. Like boarding up windows:
Tornado, tornado, now the siren…
my heart is singing as the sky turns
black. Your mouth is turning like a sign.
Sit here beside me; we can tell stories
in the dark. The dog next door pulls
at its chain, its choked yelp is mustered.
Tell me about the man who parachuted
into a storm. Your eyes are widening
as if it were you jumping; us about to leap
from the hold, the sky a bed of nails.

DARLING, MEET ME IN LANGUAGE

'Even the most tactless, blundering words are better than that 'English' silence' – K McKay

Are you scared to observe what's
in the words tangled in knots
at the back of your throat?
There a trembling, remote
riddles the tongue into silence; a sting
to us both. Can not words bring
a consolation like touch? Your hand makes
a gesture I take as a sign, but nothing takes
place, and your thumb hooks like a scythe under
your jaw – It might any moment slice
through your chin, do away with the tongue
once and for all. I watch you and wonder
how you've forgotten the price
of entry into the world, paid for when young.

I'M LOOKING AT A SUNFLOWER, LOPSIDED

in a full field of sunflowers. Each
one is a part of the overall plan
of sunflowers. Each one is a seed

in a field full of seeds,
like the skull of black seeds on each
sunflower head. I'm looking

at yellow, and at the wrap of blue
that is sky above each stem. The cape
of shadow over every one.

I'm looking at a painting by Egon Schiele
and there are no people in it,
and I realise that in paintings

by Egon Schiele, which feature people,
he paints women like awkward birds
among slight stalks of full sunflowers,

in a lopsided field. (His wife is a pigeon,
his sister is a crow – all black skull
and lopsided eye, like a seed.)

That is how close I am.